New Vanguard • 110

Universal Carrier 1936–48

The 'Bren Gun Carrier' Story

FME 862

David Fletcher • Illustrated by Tony Bryan

First published in Great Britain in 2005 by Osprey Publishing,
Midland House, West Way, Botley, Oxford OX2 0PH, UK
44-02 23rd St, Suite 219, Long Island City, NY 11101, USA
Email: info@ospreypublishing.com

Transferred to digital print on demand 2010

First published 2005
4th impression 2008

Printed and bound by Cadmus Communications, USA

A CIP catalogue record for this book is available from the British Library

ISBN: 978 1 84176 813 7

Editorial Katherine Venn
Design by Melissa Orrom Swan, Oxford, UK
Index by Glyn Sutcliffe
Originated by The Electronic Page Company, Cwmbran, UK
Typeset in Helvetica Neue and ITC New Baskerville

Editor's note
All photographs are reproduced with kind permission of the Tank Museum, Bovington.

Artist's note
Readers may care to note that the original paintings from which the colour plates in this book were prepared are available for
private sale. All reproduction copyright whatsoever is retained by the Publishers. All enquiries should be addressed to:

Tony Bryan
4a Forest View Drive
Wimborne
Dorset
BH21 7NZ
UK

The Publishers regret that they can enter into no correspondence upon this matter.

FOR A CATALOGUE OF ALL BOOKS PUBLISHED BY
OSPREY MILITARY AND AVIATION PLEASE CONTACT:

Osprey Direct, c/o Random House Distribution Center,
400 Hahn Road, Westminster, MD 21157
Email: uscustomerservice@ospreypublishing.com

Osprey Direct, The Book Service Ltd, Distribution Centre,
Colchester Road, Frating Green, Colchester, Essex, CO7 7DW
Email: customerservice@ospreypublishing.com

www.ospreypublishing.com

UNIVERSAL CARRIER 1936–48
THE 'BREN GUN CARRIER' STORY

INTRODUCTION

The Universal Carrier is typically British – peculiarly British some might say: a compromise, neither one thing nor the other. Designed for a role that it never really fulfilled, it was adapted to dozens of others for which it was never entirely suited and was still in service, in vast numbers, long after it should have been pensioned off. Granted, it was also copied by the Australian, New Zealand and Canadian armies, but presumably on the assumption that the British knew what they were doing in the first place. It saw service all over the world, with just about every army that took part in the Second World War and some that did not. It is regarded with sentimental affection by those who used it and yet it is still referred to by everyone, quite incorrectly, as the Bren Gun Carrier.

Tracked carriers were nothing new – a simple version had appeared towards the end of the Great War – but the origins of the Universal Carrier may be traced to the Ford T-powered Carden-Loyd machines of the mid-twenties, and specifically the definitive Mark VI model of 1927. When the Carden-Loyd Company was taken over by Vickers-Armstrongs in 1928 the tiny machine-gun carrier became a major component of the British Army and a considerable export success. Yet for all that it was cramped, vulnerable and unreliable with just the one merit – it was cheap.

Prototype carrier VAD50 in its original form with the coil spring on the leading bogie sloping backwards. Like the earlier Carden-Loyds, this prototype carrier had left-hand drive and a machine gun elevated by the gunner's feet. The backrests on the track guards are folded down.

Other lines of development, stemming from the Carden-Loyd, were a family of light tanks and a range of artillery tractors known as Dragons, which, on account of their greater weight, required bigger engines and a more substantial and flexible suspension system devised by the Horstman company. Most Dragons employed a Meadows six-cylinder petrol engine and in addition to their use by the British Army they enjoyed considerable success on the export market. However, they were expensive, specialized machines, and in an effort to produce something cheaper Vickers-Armstrongs launched an interesting new vehicle with the development number D50, in 1934.

Vickers-Armstrongs D50

The vehicle was delivered to the Mechanisation Experimental Establishment (MEE) at Farnborough and tested in 1935. Outwardly it did not look very exciting. The body was limited to a two-man compartment at the front, while narrow seats, running lengthways along the track guards at the rear, would accommodate the rest of the crew. Mechanically it was equally simple. The engine, located centrally in the body, was the standard commercial Ford V-8 linked by a four-speed and reverse gearbox, also by Ford, to the same company's standard truck rear axle at the back. The suspension was similar to that used on contemporary Light Dragons, the so-called Horstman slow-motion system that Vickers referred to as their 'double spring' type; however, in this case it amounted to just one and a half bogies per side. What made the design outstanding was the steering system.

One problem that had plagued the Carden-Loyds, and the Dragons, was a phenomenon known as reverse steering. This could result in a vehicle that was travelling downhill actually turning the opposite way from that intended, sometimes with disastrous results. It was a common failing with clutch and brake steering, although experienced drivers

Machine Gun Carrier No. 1 Mark I viewed from the rear with the engine panels raised to reveal the Ford V8. The rear compartment is wide open on this side but enclosed by a vertical panel on the other. T1833 (numbered as a Tank in the War Office system then in use) was later converted to become the prototype Mortar Carrier.

could use it to their advantage. The new system, which was probably the brainchild of Sir John Carden, Vickers' chief AFV designer, and of his deputy Leslie Little, was ingenious and relatively foolproof. It was so arranged that the foremost suspension units on each side shared a common axle, a strong tubular shaft that ran across the floor of the vehicle and was capable of sliding sideways to a limited extent. Activated by a steering wheel, it had the effect of displacing both bogies sideways, bending the tracks and causing the vehicle to steer, without braking or skidding, for large radius turns. Skid steering could be brought into play for tighter turns by giving a harder twist to the steering wheel; this applied a brake to one side of the differential or the other and so, since no clutch was involved, there was no risk of reverse steering.

Another advantage sometimes put forward for this system was that, by offsetting the suspension to some extent, it would allow the vehicle to run straight along a cambered road without continually trying to work its way into the gutter. The suspension system also gave a good ride across country, while the short pitch, manganese-iron tracks were hard-wearing and free-running at speed. MEE tested D50 as a light artillery tractor and a carrier for the Vickers machine gun. In the former role it evolved into the Dragon, Light, Mark III, which does not concern us here, and in the latter into an experimental machine-gun carrier, which does. The original D50 vehicle was never purchased for military service. Its suspension was subsequently modified and, later still, it appeared in an exotic camouflage scheme, mounting a Vickers 40mm anti-tank/anti-aircraft gun and offered for export.

THE MACHINE GUN CARRIERS

Within a year Vickers-Armstrongs supplied a second vehicle, this time to a War Office contract, which was referred to as an Experimental

Not all of the Machine Gun Carriers No. 2 Mark II were rebuilt as Bren Gun Carriers when the war began. Here T2600, an early Thornycroft-built example, still features a Vickers gun in the enlarged gunner's compartment as it leads a column of carriers through Amesbury, Wiltshire. The markings suggest that they are playing the part of enemy vehicles in an exercise.

Armoured Machine Gun Carrier. Identical to D50 in terms of engine, transmission and suspension, it was, more logically for a British vehicle, given a right-hand drive layout. It still retained the rear seats above the track guards but these were now provided with folding backrests and in the upright position offered seating for four men, two per side. To the left of the driver was the sixth crew member, who operated the Vickers machine gun, but stowage was also provided for six service rifles for the entire crew.

The vehicle was designed in line with recommendations published in 1935 entitled *Notes on Infantry Experiments*, which called for a carrier with 6mm armour protection, small and inconspicuous but capable of carrying a Vickers gun that could be fired either from the vehicle or, dismounted with its crew, from a tripod. It arrived at MEE in December 1935 and was subsequently modified to other roles. Following trials of this vehicle, a contract for 13 more was issued to Vickers-Armstrongs in April 1936: these were designated Carrier, Machine Gun, No. 1 Mark I and at this stage it seems that the intended role had been settled. No seats were provided on the track guards but a small compartment, protected by a raised outer hull plate, was created on the left for a third crew member. Thus there is the driver, sitting front right, the machine-gunner to his left and the third man behind him. The machine-gun mounting appears to have been more substantial and often came fitted with an extra shield, all of which suggests that the intention was to carry and fight the weapon on the vehicle.

Seven of these vehicles were subsequently modified as prototypes for other roles and the first of them, the Carrier Machine Gun No. 2 Mark I, introduced a significant new feature. This was an enlarged gunner's compartment at the front so that it stood out, like an angular bay, onto the glacis plate. It may have blocked the driver's view to his left to some extent but it made it much easier for the gunner to handle his weapon and, with its raised upper section, increased his protection. Armour on production machines was 12mm thick.

The Carrier, No. 2 Mark I was the first example to enter mass production, which could only be achieved by bringing in more manufacturers. This also accorded with a government scheme, engendered by the possibility of war, to involve more firms in defence work. Thus production of these carriers ran to over 1,100 vehicles built by Thornycroft, Morris-Motors and the road-roller manufacturer Aveling-Barford in addition to Vickers-Armstrongs.

Before moving on to the next stage it is worth taking a brief look at various experiments carried out with the first batch of Machine Gun Carriers, the No. 1 Mark I. In 1936 the original War Office machine came back to MEE in the guise of the Armoured General Scout Vehicle. Described as an 'inconspicuous high speed light tracked vehicle with a good cross-country performance for cavalry reconnaissance', it featured an enlarged compartment on the left for the second crew member, who was designated the commander/gunner. In fact he was more even than that for, in addition to firing a Bren light machine gun or Boys anti-tank rifle, as required, he was also operator of the No. 1 wireless set. The Bren was mounted at the front, where the Vickers gun would otherwise be, while the Boys rifle was clamped to a rail, running around the top of the compartment, along which it could slide to any position required. Quite where the wireless set went is not clear; they were bulky things in those days and there seems to have been precious little room, but if it was not stowed in the front compartment it is difficult to imagine how the operator would be able to get at it.

This was, of course, an era when the future of the British cavalry was being evaluated. Some regiments had already abandoned their horses

The prototype Cavalry Carrier photographed from the rear. Padded squabs and backrest for the rear passengers can be seen along with the frame for its canvas hood. There is a large locker at the back and two more above the engine, one of which has clips for the men's rifles.

for armoured cars but others were clearly being considered for a mounted infantry role, albeit mechanized. Two options were on the table; one, which was tested by the 3rd Hussars, involved lightly armoured Morris trucks that carried the men and their rifles; the other considered tracked vehicles and, in September 1936, Vickers-Armstrongs converted another Machine Gun Carrier to the new role of Cavalry Carrier. It was an odd design by any standards, intended to carry eight men and their rifles, with a Bren gun at the front and a Boys anti-tank rifle for dismounted use. The front end was configured like the Machine Gun Carrier but the rear reverted to the idea of using the track guards as seats for six more men who perched, three per side, facing one another across the engine. There was no superstructure at the rear, just a selection of stowage lockers, but in an effort to protect the men from the elements a canvas cover was available, supported by a frame.

A second Machine Gun Carrier was converted to the same role but the original example, T1830, was issued to the 9th Royal Lancers in 1937 for user trials. Here it was discovered that heat from the engine proved very unpleasant for those men seated at the back so the vehicle was modified and then passed on to Messrs Nuffield Mechanisation & Aero Ltd in Birmingham, who produced 50 service machines in 1938.

Two more from the first batch of Machine Gun Carriers were reworked as prototypes of the new Scout Carrier while a further two appeared as experimental Mortar and Equipment Carriers. Little is known about these two but the fact that they went to MEE together suggests that the plan was that they should operate as a pair. The 3in mortar was just then coming into service. It required a team of four or five and it may well be that the two carriers between them were intended to carry the weapon, its crew and a useful supply of ammunition. On the other hand it does seem an extravagant way of transporting the weapon and may explain why, for the present at least, the mortar carrier was not developed.

The Vickers 2-pdr Anti-Tank Carrier with the front crew section fully closed down. The conical gun shield is fixed to the hull while the gun, with an internal shield that moves with it, has limited traverse. The small, triangular plate on the side reveals that, despite appearances, this vehicle is unarmoured.

The last of these experimental machines, which was newly built rather than a conversion, was the Carrier, 2-Pounder, Anti-Tank. Built by Vickers-Armstrongs to a contract dated December 1936, it mounted the British Army's 2-pdr rather than Vickers' own weapon, as used on the rebuilt VAD50. It went to MEE in February 1938 and appears to have performed very well despite the additional weight. The weapon was mounted above the engine, behind a large, curved shield; it had a traverse of 20 degrees either side of dead centre, elevation of 15 degrees and depression of 10 degrees. It had a crew of four. The driver and commander sat at the front, beneath hinged hatches that could be closed down to protect them from blast when the gun fired. The gunner and loader sat behind the gun shield and the latter had access to a modest amount of stowed ammunition.

The vehicle was passed to the 9th Lancers for user trials. The only fault that MEE had been able to find was a tendency for dust, thrown up at speed, to be sucked back into the gun area owing to the aerodynamic shape of the shield, but they were convinced that this could be cured. Even so, no more were built and it seems a pity. Those cavalry regiments that used light tanks and carriers in France in 1940 could have made good use of a self-propelled anti-tank gun and there was no finer weapon than the British 2-pdr in its day. In the end it was left to the Australians and Canadians to mount 2-pdr guns on carriers later in the war, but these were never used either.

THE BREN GUN CARRIER

So much for the experimental era. In 1935 the British Army adopted a new light machine gun, the Bren Gun, to replace the venerable Lewis gun. Based upon a Czech design, it weighed 28lbs (12.6kg) and could easily be carried by one man. In 1930 the Chief of the Imperial General Staff, Field Marshal Sir George Milne, suggested that a new, general- purpose machine gun be developed that was lighter than the Lewis gun but capable of a sustained rate of fire as good as, if not better than, the venerable Vickers. This latter requirement proved impossible to fulfil so an alternative plan was devised. The heavy Vickers would be taken away from infantry

A Thornycroft-built Bren Gun Carrier from the very first batch showing the folding, sloped plate at the rear of the third crew member's compartment. The tool on the left side is the track-adjusting bar; pickaxe, shovel and tow rope are located at the back.

battalions and formed into independent battalions, not unlike the Machine Gun Corps of the First World War. Meanwhile, the Bren gun would be issued to the infantry and employed down to platoon level.

The .303in Vickers machine gun required at least three men to carry it and even then was quite a handful with its tripod, water canister and ammunition boxes. Yet, from 1937 onwards, the Carrier, Machine Gun, was adapted to carry the Bren instead and by the end of that year contracts were being placed for the Carrier, Bren, and many of the original vehicles were being reworked. The first contract to name the Bren Carrier specifically was one placed with the Sentinel Waggon Company in November 1937, but the earlier contracts for Machine Gun Carriers No. 2 were all amended to include Bren Gun Carriers at some stage in production. The machine-gun battalions, meanwhile, were issued with 15cwt trucks. The logic behind this was that the vehicle that carried the Bren gun would be in the forward area and, although it was not intended to fight from within the vehicle, it could at least operate in the front line with some degree of protection. The Vickers, on the other hand, would be further back and, in the transport stage at least, less vulnerable, so that unarmoured transport would suffice.

The use of the Bren Gun Carrier within the infantry battalion was laid out in a War Office pamphlet of 1940. Ten carriers were supplied to each battalion, and incorporated into a Carrier Platoon (Number 4 Platoon) of the battalion's headquarters company. Within the carrier platoon nine of the carriers were organized into three sections, obviously of three carriers per section. The tenth carrier would be attached to platoon headquarters.

Each Bren Carrier carried three men: a driver and two others who formed the Bren Gun Detachment. One carrier per section also carried a Boys anti-tank rifle. It is worth pointing out that each section in a rifle company also had one Bren Gun so that they were by no means exclusive to the carrier platoon. The pamphlet went on to point out that the carrier was only bullet-proof up to a point and that its cross-country mobility, while good, had limitations. For example it would not just be defeated by anti-tank obstacles, but often by other obstacles that tanks could cope with. The battalion commander was urged to keep these aspects in mind when using the vehicles in action.

The emphasis appears to have been on dismounted use of the Bren Gun and much was made of the fact that the weapon crew must be able to dismount in a hurry, permitting the carrier to withdraw to a place of safety while they went into the firing line. On no account was the driver permitted to leave his vehicle. Firing from the carrier was entirely possible and early models had a special bracket which attached to the front mounting of the machine gun and a sort of crutch

Machine Gun Carriers No. 2 Mark I that do not appear to have been modified to the Bren role being used for driver training early in the war. Having everyone wear gas masks undoubtedly helps to make it all that little bit more difficult.

that supported the rear end. On later models the Bren was not physically attached to the vehicle, merely resting on a rubber block in the weapon slot and held in place by the gunner. Taking advantage of their mobility, the carriers normally operated on the flanks of the battalion but they were expected to keep in close touch with one another and a scheme of signalling by red and blue flags was laid down in the pamphlet.

A TASTE OF WAR

No better example can be found of the aggressive use of carriers than the instance of the platoon from 1st Battalion, Welsh Guards during the breakout from Arras. The Welsh Guards had gone to France as General Headquarters (GHQ) troops in the British Expeditionary Force (BEF) and when the German attack began they were part of the garrison at Arras. The city had been reinforced for a counter-attack by 1st Army Tank Brigade on 21 May 1940 but since this failed it was agreed that evacuation was the only answer.

The early morning of 24 May brought a thick mist, under cover of which the various forces dispersed. One section of three Bren Carriers under Lieutenant the Honourable Christopher Furness undertook to escort the regimental transport but, within a few miles, ran into enemy positions. It would take time to turn the column of trucks around, leaving them vulnerable once the mist lifted, so Furness decided to keep the Germans busy while the lorries escaped. Supported by a few light tanks Furness led the carrier section towards the German position, which proved to be well sited and effectively defended. Anti-tank guns soon disposed of the British tanks but the nippy little carriers proved to be more elusive targets. Circling the enemy position, like Indians attacking a wagon train, they inflicted some casualties but in the end there could be but one result.

Having lost his driver and gunner, Furness, in the leading carrier, dismounted and launched a one-man attack during which he was killed in hand-to-hand fighting. With the second carrier also out of action, the third withdrew to sort out a damaged Bren gun. That done, they returned to the attack, only to be halted by an anti-tank gun. In the end, of the nine men, four were killed, four wounded and one taken prisoner.

Scout Carriers of a divisional reconnaissance regiment of the British Expeditionary Force, some with Bren guns rigged for anti-aircraft defence. The rearmost vehicle has an aerial base, indicating that it is equipped with a wireless set.

Furness was awarded a posthumous Victoria Cross, probably the first VC to be earned by carrier troops.

The Scout Carrier

The Bren Carrier was not supposed to be employed as an assault vehicle. It was seen as a weapon carrier for dismounted action. The Scout Carrier, on the other hand, was regarded as a fighting vehicle. It was intended for issue to mechanized cavalry regiments acting in the divisional reconnaissance role and each such regiment had 28 light tanks and 44 Scout Carriers.

Prototypes of this model have already been mentioned but the production version, of which some 600 were built by Nuffields and Aveling-Barford, requires description. In mechanical terms it was identical to the Bren, as was the front crew compartment, but at the rear it was quite different, being virtually a mirror image. The rear crew compartment was on the right side of the engine, not the left, and the stowage lockers were transposed to the left side. However, it did not end there. The crew compartment was larger and squared off at the back so, viewed from the right side, it was actually difficult to tell apart from a Universal Carrier. The reason for the enlarged compartment was the requirement to carry a radio and its extra batteries but there is no obvious reason why the different layout was adopted. The radio was the No. 11 set but in the BEF these were limited to one in every three carriers. Also, at least ideally, the Scout Carrier operated with a Boys anti-tank rifle in the front weapon slit and the Bren gun on a pintle at the back, fired by the radio operator.

The divisional cavalry regiments were organized as three squadrons, each of which comprised a squadron headquarters that included two light tanks and two carriers, plus two troops of light tanks and four of carriers: three vehicles per troop. Regimental headquarters had four light tanks and two carriers. Finding accounts of any stirring actions from this period is an unrewarding task. Mostly one gets excuses. The 15th/19th King's Royal Hussars point out that by January 1940 most of

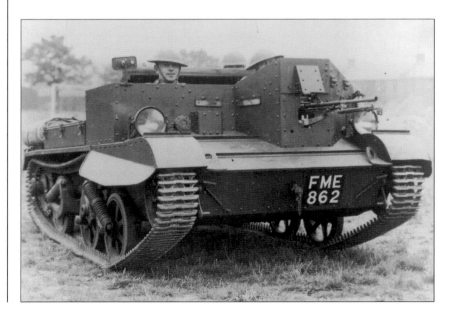

A Bren Carrier that started life as a Machine Gun Carrier No. 2 Mark I. The support for the Bren gun shows up well as do the protected visors for the driver and gunner. The plug in the nose plate, just inboard of the registration number, covers the hole for the engine starting handle.

their vehicles had time-expired engines that only kept going because of the quality of British workmanship. They claim that track wear was only alleviated by having two sets per vehicle: training tracks for everyday use and new battle tracks, to be fitted when the time came.

The 5th Royal Inniskilling Dragoon Guards paint an even worse picture. Dismissing the Boys anti-tank rifles as 'small-arms' for all the good they were, and having slated the light tanks, their historian goes on to say:

> In this mobile warfare the unfortunate Bren [sic] Carrier troops were in an even worse position, equipped as they were to do no more than hold ground against infantry and light vehicles – very light vehicles at that. In the whole regiment we could muster no weapon which could be sure of penetrating a German Panzer . . .

Clearly the difference between a Bren and a Scout Carrier was lost on the 'Skins'. Not that it mattered in the end: after a few days of confusion and combat the survivors were all making for Dunkirk, abandoning such vehicles as remained.

Overhead view of a Universal Carrier Mark I displaying crew seats and basic stowage. The driver's steering wheel and gear-change can be seen while the track-adjusting tool is located across the front plate. External fittings on the hull side are, from the rear, a wireless aerial base, anti-aircraft mount for a Bren gun and the bracket that holds a 4in smoke grenade discharger.

In passing, there is evidence that some Cavalry Carriers served in France with 1st Army Tank Brigade (4th and 7th Battalions, Royal Tank Regiment), which reputedly employed them as spare crew carriers for their tanks. It is also clear from photographs that, when 52nd (Lowland) Division was rushed over to France in the last days, as French resistance flickered out, they had Universal Carriers with them.

Finally, at this stage, it remains to record one other type, the Carrier Armoured Observation Post Mark I, of which 95 were built by Aveling-Barford in 1939. These were Scout Carriers in outward appearance but distinguished by a cable reel fitted at the rear and a protected slot that replaced the gun aperture in the front compartment. This slot was designed to accommodate binoculars so that the artillery Forward Observation Officer (FOO) could spot for his battery, remain in touch by radio or landline and enjoy some mobility and protection at the same time. Such vehicles would be issued to the Royal Artillery but whether any went to France has not been established.

In the aftermath of the defeat in France, a committee under General Sir William Bartholomew sat to consider the lessons. Many of the findings, on reconnaissance and the use of wireless for example, could be applied to carriers, but where they are specific it appears that they were thinking of the carrier in the infantry role: 'The Carrier was a great success even when used in the assault role, for which it was never intended. There was a general demand for increased numbers by all arms, and for many purposes.' The Carrier, it seems, was becoming Universal by default.

Among the committee's specific recommendations were an increase in the number of carriers to four per platoon and that provision should be made to enable the anti-tank rifle to be aimed backwards. Smoke grenades should be carried but a 2in mortar was suggested as an alternative and an anti-aircraft mounting for the Bren gun was required. On the subject of the carrier platoon in an infantry battalion, the report said:

> The Carrier Platoon provides the Battalion Commander with a reserve of firepower and the means with which to carry out a counter-attack . . . [Carriers] proved of immense value in every role, mounted, dismounted or when driven across the front without firing to frighten enemy infantry.

THE UNIVERSAL CARRIER

Another recommendation of the Bartholomew Committee, in respect of carriers, said: 'Armour should be raised by two or three inches especially at the back.' In this they had been anticipated, up to a point. The logic behind a Universal Carrier was incontestable: one basic design that could be adapted to a variety of roles made a lot more sense than a range of different vehicles.

The first contracts for Universal Carriers, specifically named as such, had been dated 1 April 1939 and amounted to 2,275 vehicles shared between Aveling-Barford, Sentinel Waggon, Nuffield and Thornycroft. Larger orders followed in September, all of which would take time to fill, and there would be changes during production. The suggestion that late production Bren or Scout Carriers were completed as Universals is not borne out by the contract cards, nor is there any hard evidence for Brens or Scouts being rebuilt as Universals. Numbers are against it; they were in considerable demand and soon virtually worn out so it would have been less trouble to build new machines.

Scout Carriers in the Middle East. Most have Boys rifles at the front and a Bren at the back. All appear to be equipped with radio. There is no sign here of the extra stowage that soon characterized most British vehicles in North Africa.

Indian troops with an exotically camouflaged Universal Carrier learn how to co-operate with their newly mechanized platoon in Eritrea. This particular vehicle was built by Wolseley Motors. It has what may be two strips of spare track stowed across the front.

The first edition of the handbook that mentions the Universal Carrier, issued in December 1940, describes it thus:

> The general construction of the hull is a combination of the Bren and Scout Carriers but with protection plates on both sides and at the rear. No rear flap is fitted. The engine cover is of modified design having bullet-proof plates on the top only, the side plates being of mild steel, and easily detachable. Provision is made on all machines for a No. 11 wireless set. The machine can function as a Bren or Scout Carrier.

In other words the body was totally enclosed at sides and rear and the engine completely boxed in with a flat armoured plate over the top and vertical side panels. On 10 September 1939, six days after war against Germany was declared, four more orders were placed with the same four contractors, although this time the Nuffield contract was more specific and named Wolseley Motors. Each order was for 1,000 Universal Carriers Mark I. No more contracts were issued until the following June (before the disaster at Arras), when 2,800 were ordered, and then November 1940, when contracts were placed for a further 2,937, an odd figure. Of these, 400 from the Wolseley contract were completed as Three-Inch Mortar Carriers. Parallel with the September 1939 and June 1940 orders are two contracts with Aveling-Barfords for, respectively, 253 and 493 Carriers Armoured OP Mark II. A third contract for 316 of the same, to match the November 1940 contracts is marked 'Cancelled'. There is no space to list more, suffice it to say that by 1942 a further 6,600 Mark I Carriers were supplied from the same British manufacturers, along with an increasing number of Three-Inch Mortar Carriers.

The distinction of armoured vehicles by Mark is extremely common and with some types, particularly tanks, it can be very significant. Where carriers are concerned it is minimal but, just for variety, there is another distinction. This concerns the engine. In all cases the engines fitted were the standard Ford V8 of the day but three, later four, different types were supplied. These were: the type 79E, the British engine rated at 65hp, the American GAE/GAEA, both rated at 85hp, and the Canadian COIUC of

95hp. However, the American engines were reworked in Britain for use in carriers and carried the designations EGAE and EGAEA. The difference was not significant although, whereas the parts for American and Canadian engines were interchangeable, the British model was not.

In order to identify the engine type in each carrier an extra designator was added. Thus a carrier with the British engine was styled Carrier, Universal No. 1 Mark I; with the first American engine, No. 2 Mark I; with the EGAEA engine, No. 2A Mark I; and with the Canadian engine, No. 3 Mark I. And these designations applied to all subsequent marks and types of carrier.

Middle East

According to the British Official History the army in Egypt was desperately short of everything in 1940, and this included 500 carriers. The reason was, naturally, that the army in France had priority. However 7th Armoured Division had a share of the Scout Carriers and it is clear from photographs that Bren Gun Carriers were available to the infantry. The arrival of Dominion and Commonwealth troops put an additional strain on supplies. For example, although plans were in place to bring Indian divisions up to the standard of their British counterparts this had still not been done when they arrived in the Middle East, so the first step was to place troops in camps in the Delta and train them on the new equipment, which would include carriers. A similar situation greeted the arrival of Australian and New Zealand troops. For example, 6th Australian Divisional Cavalry Regiment, when it first arrived in the Middle East, should have had the British establishment of 28 light tanks and 44 Scout Carriers. Nothing like this number was available and when A Squadron, the first Australian armoured unit ever to see action, took part in the attack on Bardia only twenty carriers were provided and they were poor ones in a worn-out state. To overcome the firepower deficit

Australian troops with a rather battered Mark I Universal in Syria. A Vickers water-cooled machine gun, for which the front weapon slot must have been enlarged, is seen, complete with the hose that links to the carrier's cooling system. Not content with that, the driver had a Boys rifle, the radio operator a Bren and the gunner a Thompson sub-machine gun.

caused by the lack of light tanks, the Australians modified their carriers to carry a Vickers machine gun in addition to the Bren and improved things further by connecting up the Vickers gun's water-cooling system with the carrier's radiator.

Things had improved to some extent when the New Zealand Division first saw action and they appear to have been particularly aggressive in their use of carriers. During actions along the Alamein Line in the summer of 1942 their 19th Battalion sent their reserve carrier section out on a patrol from which only one returned. The other two were last seen departing in a hurry, pursued by Axis tanks. In fact they outran the tanks and later joined up with some British armoured cars, although by that time one carrier was towing the other, which was suffering from a defunct generator. After spending three nights in the desert with various British units, having been shot up by the Luftwaffe and travelled well over a hundred miles they repaired the inoperative carrier from a wreck and ultimately rejoined the Battalion.

That the Universal Carrier and its predecessors earned their popularity in the desert, although they were often misused and abused, goes without saying. Abuse took many forms; overloading was one. The Universal Carrier was deemed to have a payload of 13cwt (660kg) but even in everyday use this was often exceeded. For one thing, nobody ever bothered to weigh what was being loaded. Misuse was due in part to popularity: everyone wanted them for every purpose, and wanted to use them in combat for activities that did not suit them, simply because nothing else was available. For example, tank regiments often operated a reconnaissance troop of carriers and then complained because they were not adequately armoured. In the later stages of the desert campaign many British regiments removed the turrets from their Stuart tanks and employed them for reconnaissance, in effect creating large, well-armoured carriers.

User demand would lead to many improvements. The ability to deploy smoke, for example, caused many crews to stow a 2in mortar aboard and fire it from the engine cover plate if required. In the open desert a Bren gun trapped in a slot at the front was not popular; all-round defence was

Typical of the small business premises throughout Britain that took on the task of improving Mark I Carriers, this unidentified location permits comparison of 'before' and 'after' examples in the street. Notice on the latter the change of headlight arrangements, front stowage for the spare road wheel and towing cable, and the split steel tubing, rounding off the edges of the main fighting compartment.

required so there was a cry for more flexibility in how the weapon could be mounted and used. At the same time, crews were demanding an anti-aircraft mount. Most of these requirements were met in due course but, since additional armour was a problem, crews improvised, at least against mines, by lining the vehicle's floor with filled sandbags. It may have reduced the effect of blast but it added to the weight. Full length sand shields, probably locally made, are seen on some carriers in the theatre at this time.

The desert imposed its own pressures. The Ford V8 has always been regarded as an excellent power unit but it had its limits. The engine itself, the gearbox and the driving axle were all designed for a wheeled vehicle, and an unarmoured one at that. Tracked vehicles are never as free-rolling as wheeled machines; their violent methods of steering send shocks back through the transmission and the very fact that they can operate over rough ground exacerbates the punishment. The driver's immediate answer to any problem is to try to power through, which does the most willing engine no good at all, nor the transmission come to that. The result was an epidemic of failures of head gaskets and big ends, together with collapsed pistons and excessive wear to all parts. Gearboxes seized, gear selector forks bent and broke or driving axles developed oil leaks. In such an abrasive environment it is not surprising that the exposed steering system suffered wear or that tracks stretched and broke, while overloading led to suspension collapse and to rubber tyres coming away from wheels. Major William Blagden, examining an overturned carrier in Tunisia, noted how the twin exhaust pipes beneath the hull floor had been beaten almost flat by constant blows on uneven ground.

If this sounds like a catalogue of failure, it is in reality only normal wear and tear under the circumstances, and with the excellent back-up provided by the Royal Army Ordnance Corps (RAOC), and later the Royal Electrical and Mechanical Engineers (REME), the carriers were always there to continue the fight.

Actor Richard Greene, Robin Hood to a generation of TV viewers, photographed in the gunner's position of a very badly knocked about Cavalry Carrier as part of his training in the Royal Tank Regiment. The pivoting backrests for the rear crew members can be seen along with the shield that prevented coat tails or personal equipment becoming caught in the tracks when on the move.

Defence of Britain

The precise number of carriers lost in France cannot be calculated because it is not entirely clear how many went out there in the first place. One can calculate how many there ought to have been but that would not include replacements or reserve stocks. Yet it would be safe to say that a minimum figure would be in the region of 1,000.

The situation in Britain, even before the final collapse of France, was clearly critical. It was not a shortage of men, but of equipment, that posed the real problem. Tanks in particular were only trickling out from the factories and some regiments had just one or two old ones to train on. On the principle that anything was better than nothing, three Yeomanry regiments, 1st Gloucestershire Hussars together with 1st and 2nd Northamptonshire Yeomanry, were each required to provide one squadron to form – in the same order – X, Y and Z Squadrons of the Yeomanry Armoured Detachment. It was an odd set-up, equipped with a handful of Light Tanks, Guy Armoured Cars, Scout Carriers and a few new Universal Carriers. It was based at Newmarket and kept on short notice to turn out and resist a German landing on the coast of East Anglia. The threat of air attack, which had so affected troops in France, resulted in the Detachment's Universal Carriers being fitted with armoured roofs, covering the entire open body of the vehicle. All this achieved in practice was to turn them into death traps, since it would have been very difficult for the crews to dismount in a hurry.

The Yeomanry Armoured Detachment was effectively disbanded by the end of May since the errant squadrons each rejoined their respective regiments, all of which now moved down to Kent as 20th Armoured Brigade once again. Not that they were finished with carriers. Apart from 2nd Northamptonshire Yeomanry, which became an armoured car regiment for the duration, the other two acquired even more carriers and did not receive tanks until the last quarter of the year.

The Prime Minister does his best to look comfortable in the rear seat of a Universal Carrier named for his illustrious ancestor. This vehicle, built by Sentinel, is still in its original state but provides an excellent view of the 2in mortar mounted, it seems, on the engine cover.

Improved carriers

As already noted, production was expanding rapidly and in 1942 an improved model was introduced. This was the Mark II, of which British manufacturers produced some 11,000. These were the same firms as before, less Vickers-Armstrongs of course, but now including Ford of Britain. Not that Ford were new to carrier work. Their first contract for Armoured Observation Post (AOP) Carriers dates back to September 1941 and this appears to have been all they built until a contract, dated August 1942, was issued. According to the card it was originally for 3,346 Carriers Three-Inch Mortar but it appears to have been altered on War Office instructions to 3,761 Carriers Universal No. 1 Mark II 'welded hull'.

The Mark II Universal Carrier is described variously in official sources. The January 1943 issue of the Service Instruction Book states:

> The Mark II has a crew of four, two in the front compartment and two seats in the rear of the hull, one either side.
> The front quarter of the top track run is totally enclosed by a valance.
> Four foot steps are provided, two each side of the vehicle.
> A spare wheel and tow rope are fitted across the front of the vehicle.
> A large kit box fits transversely across the rear of the hull.
> It is worth noting that in fitting a spare wheel at the front it was necessary to rearrange the headlights.

A later edition merely says of the Mark II: 'Basically Mark I but restowed and embodying modifications e.g. initial water-proofing.' This presumably refers to an increased use of welding in the hull assembly process that would create a watertight joint without any additional work.

The Bren gunner on this 8th Army Universal Carrier engages a target while a second man spots for him. Typical of the desert warriors, this carrier is so overloaded with extra stores, both inside and out, that it is almost impossible to tell what it is; but out here if you desire creature comforts you must take them with you.

In November 1943 a contract card with Sentinel refers to Carriers Universal No 1 Mk II (W.T.), implying that the radio fit was a special feature of this batch. Even as production of the new model started, a major programme was initiated to bring Mark I Carriers up to Mark II standard. It would appear that numerous small firms all over the country were involved and photographic evidence suggests that the conversion did not include the new valance since the converted examples are shown still fitted with the older pattern described in the instruction book as an angular mud deflector.

The Universal Carrier Mark III, which still came (in theory at least) with the four engine options, is listed in later editions of the handbook and identified as 'Mark II but with modified air inlet and engine cover'. Only one complete contract can be found, dated simply 1943, with the Ford Motor Company. It clearly began as Mark II, the extra Roman digit being added in pencil, and was initially for 784 vehicles to which a further 608 have been added. A second contract with the same company for 3,200 No. 1 Mark III and dated July 1944 is marked 'CANCELLED'. Presumably at this stage in the war supply had started to outstrip demand.

NORTH AMERICAN PRODUCTION

Evidence for the production of regular Universal Carriers in the United States is slim and contradictory. It goes without saying that the British would have liked to order carriers from US manufacturers, and the capacity was there, but such orders would have contravened President Roosevelt's instruction that American factories should build only standard American types which the Allies could have if they wished. This was obviously relaxed later, since Ford in the USA built the larger T16 model exclusively for Britain. Even so, in some wartime British records huge batches of WD serials for Universal Carriers are clearly marked USA, which at least suggests an intention.

If not the USA then what about Canada? Here was production capacity approaching that of the United States and, arguably, a more pliable administration. Better still, the Canadian Army was organized

Although built by Sentinel as a Three-Inch Mortar Carrier, this un-stowed example provides a good view of many of the basic identification features of a Mark II Universal. The new front valance with foot step shows clearly and one can also see the holder for a water can, the bracket that holds the spare wheel and the hooks that secure the tow rope. The masked headlamp, on its special bracket, is obscured by the gunner's compartment.

along British lines and the carrier was an integral component that had to come from somewhere. Production began early in 1941, and in December 1941 a Canadian Universal Carrier T22213 was tested by MEE in direct competition with a British-built version. The investigators concluded that in terms of performance there was little to choose between them. T22213 was also used to test the effect of full-length sand guards, which proved to be perfectly satisfactory.

The establishment of production facilities in Canada was no easy matter, however. There was no local experience of the production of armour plate, for example, but a combination of trial and error with good common sense ultimately came up with a simple and economic formula, by Dofasco (Dominion Foundries and Steel), that was later adopted in Britain and America. A company with experience in straightening heavy-duty saw blades developed a technique for heat treating and flattening the plates which ultimately ended up with the Dominion Bridge Co in Windsor, Ontario, where hulls were fabricated. The entire process was controlled by the Ford Motor Company of Canada whose President, W. R. Campbell, appointed a young engineer named Jim Ronson to oversee the project. Production vehicles began to appear in February 1941. Canadian-built Universal Carriers were all fitted with the American 85hp Ford V8 rather than the 95hp Canadian type and were consequently classified No. 2 Mark I*, the asterisk indicating a Canadian-produced vehicle.

From 1943 production switched to an improved model, the No. 2 Mark II*. This was virtually identical with the British version except that extra holes were provided for easy conversion to the Ronson flame-thrower role and, rather than use rubber mounting blocks as weapon rests along the top edges of the hull, the Canadians came up with a simple alternative: a split mild steel pipe. Canadian sources claim that this model had seats for four in the rear, giving a total seating capacity of six, but this is not evident from surviving photographs or drawings.

For some reason, many of these carriers, intended for service with Allied forces in North Africa, were completed with what was known, at the time, as 'Welch Guards' stowage. Quite why is not clear beyond the obvious implication that it had been devised by the Welsh Guards for the

A Universal Carrier Mark III viewed from the rear shows the large stowage locker with the canvas holder attached, the strong Stacey towing attachment and the little square panels welded to the hull which are mounting points for the special deep-wading panels. The hull appears to be fully welded and it is finished off, around the top edge, by a simpler system of what appears to be thin plate, bent over.

carrier platoons of infantry regiments. These vehicles were also characterized by full-length track guards and an all-over canvas hood, supported by a tubular frame, which is rarely if ever seen on operational vehicles.

WITH THE INFANTRY

Although it changed in detail and increased in complexity and size as the war went on, the basic infantry division was always structured around a nucleus of three brigades, each of three infantry battalions. The original BEF establishment has already been mentioned. Following adoption of the Universal Carrier the battalion's carrier platoon expanded to four sections, each of three carriers plus one with platoon HQ. Carriers employed in this way were stowed to suit their role.

The motorized battalions, of which the infantry brigade in an armoured division was made up, were organized along precisely the same lines except that the infantry were excused foot-slogging and travelled everywhere in lorries. The Motor Battalion, on the other hand, was a much more specialized arrangement. This was an infantry battalion that formed an integral part of an armoured brigade.

The motor battalion could operate as an entity in a deliberate attack on a defended position, or when it occupied a position, or it could act as a pivot point around which armoured regiments could manoeuvre. At the time of its creation, in 1943, the assault platoons which formed the bulk of the motor battalion were carried in 15cwt platoon trucks, but when the armoured divisions went to France in 1944 the trucks had been replaced by armoured half-tracks.

What concerns us is the Scout Platoon, which comprised a platoon headquarters of two scout cars, two Universal Carriers and two motorcycles, and three sections, each of which fielded three carriers and one motorcycle. Military Training Pamphlet No. 41, the part dealing with the motor battalion, insists that the section must not be split up. Each carrier

A 'Welch Guards' Carrier with the overall canvas cover, full-length valances and raised mounting for the wireless aerial. It sports the Welsh name for Wales and the insignia of the Guards Armoured Division but the layout at the front is odd having all the fittings one would expect to find on a Mark II, with the headlamp layout of a Mark I.

Mark I Universals of the Scots Guards in a most unusual camouflage scheme. There are more vehicles here than one would expect to find in the carrier platoon of a rifle battalion but the presence of Norton 633 motorcycle sidecar units suggests an early date. Some carriers mount a Boys rifle at the front while all appear to have the pillar-mounted Bren gun and a few the 2in mortar.

had a three-man crew comprising commander, driver/mechanic and a rear gunner or wireless operator. Radio sets were provided for the platoon commander's carrier and the section commanders.

The scout platoon had three primary roles: reconnaissance of course, protection in a defensive situation and, in an assault, to provide cover for the attacking infantry and maintain a link between the advancing armour and follow-up troops. However, the pamphlet emphasizes, at regular intervals, that the scout platoon's carriers were not tanks and should never be used as such.

Three-inch Mortar Carriers

The origin of this role has already been mentioned, as have production contracts starting in 1941. The 3in mortar was in service from the outbreak of war and its adaptation to the carrier was effective from 1941. In May 1941, when the matter was still in the development stage, one idea put forward was to stow the mortar ammunition in a No. 27 Limber – the two-wheeled trailer normally associated with the 25-pdr gun. The Mechanisation Experimental Establishment (MEE) carried out towing trials in Long Valley, Aldershot. These showed that a carrier could handle the trailer perfectly well although it knocked about 3mph (4.8km/h) off the top speed and needed careful handling on wet roads, since the limber tended to take charge. In the event it was decided to carry the ammunition and the mortar in the carrier itself, which, it was calculated, increased the laden weight from 3 tons 16cwt (3,860kg) to

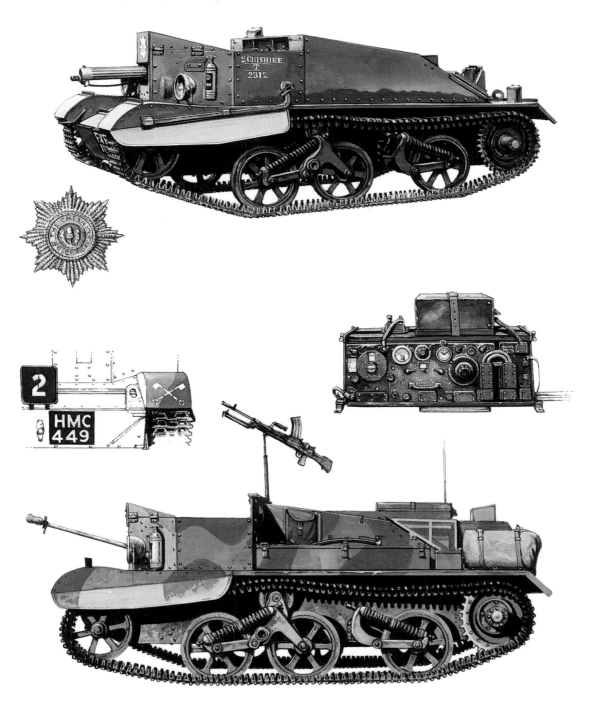

**A1: Machine Gun Carrier No. 2 Mark I, 2nd Battalion
The Cheshire Regiment, c.1937**

**A2: Scout Carrier of 4th/7th Royal Dragoon Guards,
Second Division, British Expeditionary Force, France, 1940**

B1: Bren Gun Carrier, 4th Indian Division, Egypt, 1940

**B2: Universal Carrier X Squadron (1RGH) Yeomanry
Armoured Detachment, GB, 1941**

B

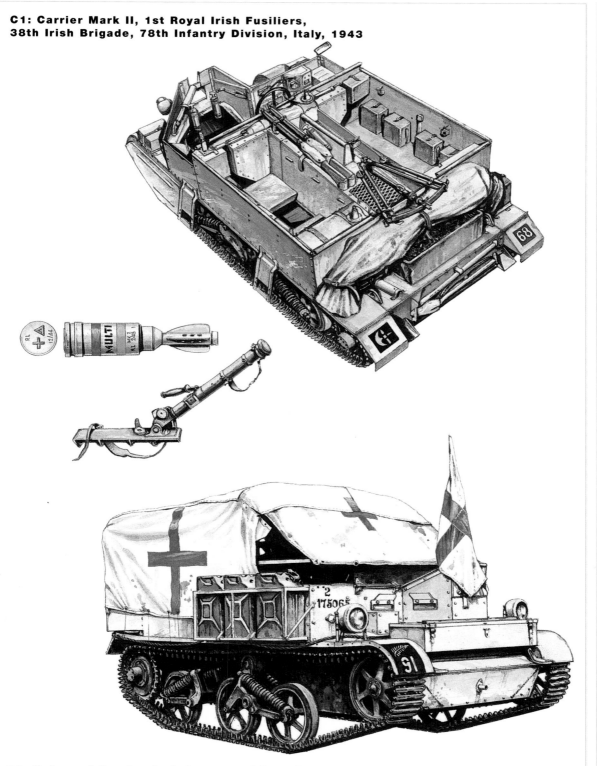

C1: Carrier Mark II, 1st Royal Irish Fusiliers, 38th Irish Brigade, 78th Infantry Division, Italy, 1943

C2: Universal Carrier Ambulance, 2nd New Zealand Division, Italy, 1943

C

D: UNIVERSAL CARRIER MARK II

KEY

1 Drive sprocket
2 Brake drum
3 Differential
4 Engine cover air inlet
5 Manifold
6 Carburettor
7 Return roller
8 Detachable pouch
9 Suspension fork
10 Control unit
11 Suspension spring
12 Road wheel
13 Gunner's seat
14 Protected vision slit
15 Weapon slot
16 Towing and lifting bracket
17 Clutch pedal
18 Brake pedal
19 Accelerator pedal
20 Handbrake lever
21 Gear selector
22 Steering fork
23 Steering column
24 Steering box
25 Steering wheel
26 Movable cross shaft
27 Gearbox link rod
28 Steering cam plate
29 Clutch link rod
30 Radiator
31 Track guard
32 Front step
33 Distributor
34 Radiator cooling fan
35 Fan belt
36 Dynamo (generator)
37 Right cylinder bank
38 Fuel pump
39 Starter motor
40 Oil filler
41 Gearbox
42 Fuel tank
43 Air filter
44 Rear step
45 Silencer
46 Ford V8 engine
47 Track idler wheel

SPECIFICATIONS

Crew 4
Combat weight 4.5 tons
Length 12ft (3.6m)
Width 7ft (2.1m)
Height 5ft 3in (1.6m)
Engine Ford V8 90-degree L head
Transmission dry single plate clutch 4-speed
and reverse selective gearbox
Fuel capacity 20 gals (90l)
Max speed 30mph (48km/h)
Max range 140 miles (225km)
Fuel consumption 7mpg
Vertical obstacle 2ft (0.6m)
Gap crossed 4ft 6in (1.3m)
Armour thickness 10mm max. 4mm min.
Armament 1x .303" Bren light machine gun,
1x Boys .55 anti-tank rifle, 1x 2in mortar or
4in smoke generator.

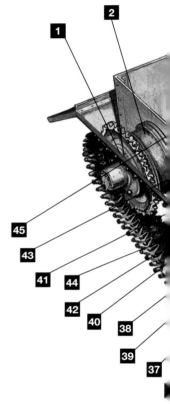

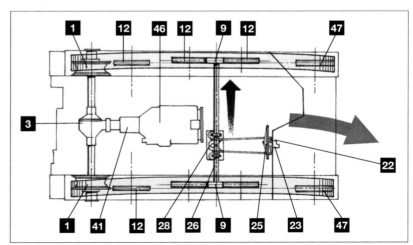

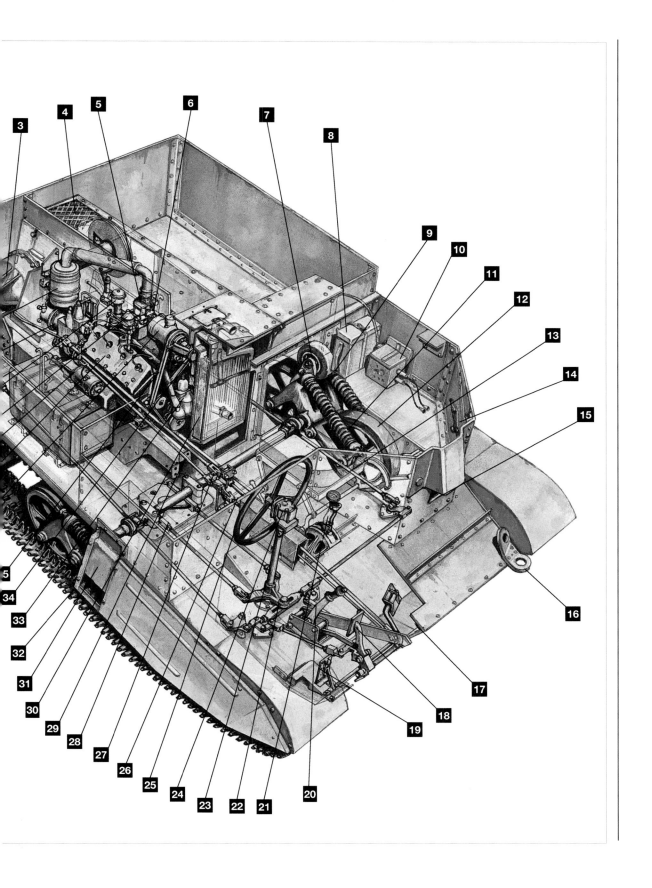

E1: Three-inch Mortar Carrier, The Royal Winnipeg Rifles, 3rd Canadian Infantry Division, UK

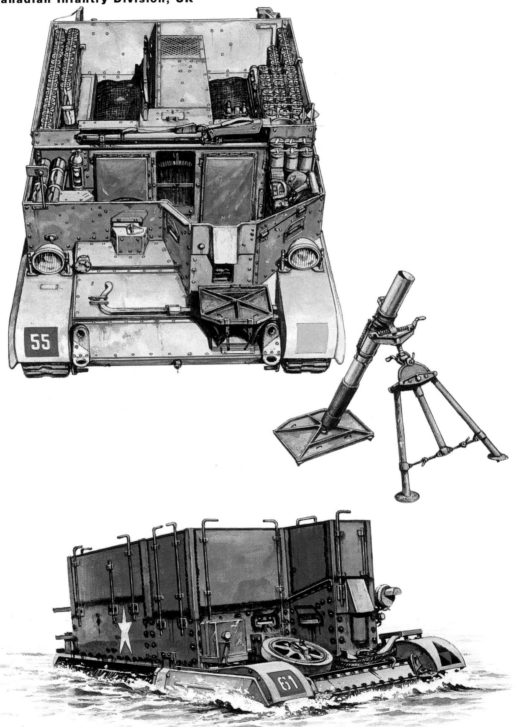

E2: Universal Carrier, 9th Infantry Brigade, 3rd Infantry Division, equipped for deep wading, D-Day 6 June 1944

F1: AOP Carrier Mark II, 1st Battery, 69th Field Regiment, 49th Infantry Division, Normandy, 1944

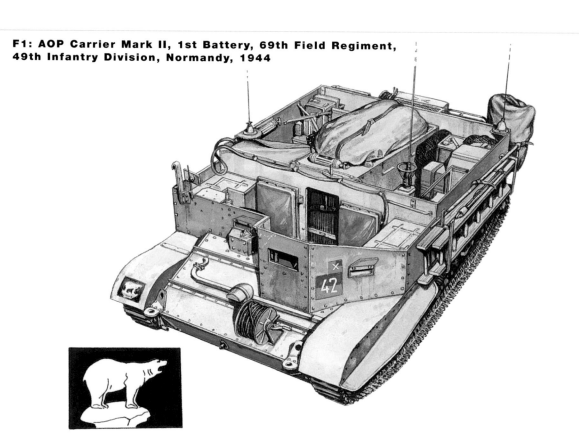

F2: Medium Machine Gun Carrier, 1st Battalion The Middlesex Regiment, 15th Scottish Division, north-west Europe, 1944

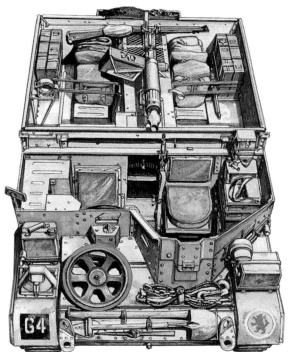

G: Universal Carriers Mark I*, Ford factory, Windsor, Ontario, 1942

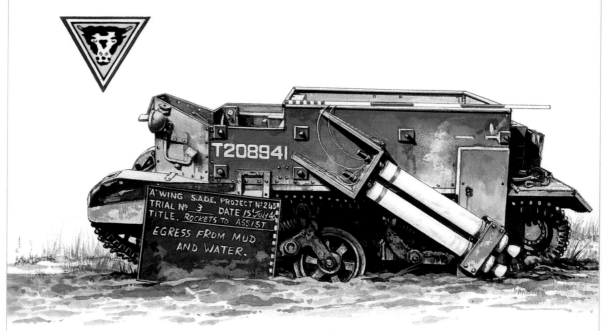

G2: Universal Carrier Mark I, Specialised Armour Development Establishment, Woodbridge, Suffolk, July 1946

4 tons 6cwt (4,368kg). MEE was concerned about this and in October 1941 carried out trials with a carrier loaded to the higher weight. This revealed greater wear on suspension units, wheels and tyres and, for the first time since carrier trials began, failure of the bogie cross-tube that effected steering.

The weapon itself, in disassembled form, was stowed across the back of the vehicle, with ammunition inside. It must have been cramped since, in addition, each Mortar Carrier was supposed to carry one NCO, a driver and three privates who had to squeeze in the back with the ammunition. A mortar platoon formed an integral part of an infantry battalion and it relied almost entirely on carriers. The lieutenant in command had one, which he shared with the driver, a REME fitter and a range taker, while his platoon comprised six detachments, each of which was a carrier equipped with one 3in mortar and 66 rounds of ammunition, both high explosive and smoke. On coming into action under normal circumstances, the crew would dismount, assemble the mortar on the ground and commence firing to order. Photographs show that attempts were made to fire the mortar from the front compartment but this would probably cause severe damage to the hull floor.

Armoured Observation Post Carriers

The original model of this variant has already been noted. Contracts for subsequent batches of 253 and 493 AOP Mark II were awarded to Aveling-Barford in September 1939 and June 1940 respectively. The contract cards imply that they were of the 'Universal Type' yet similar to the first batch, which sounds like a contradiction. They were Universal Carriers to outward appearance but similar to the first AOP model in respect of the binocular visor at the front and cable reel at the back, No. 11 radio and three-man crew. Demand must have exceeded supply if some sources are correct. For example, 86 Field Regiment, Royal Artillery, otherwise the Hertfordshire Yeomanry, received Mark I Universal carriers on the scale of

Three-Inch Mortar Carrier Mark II of the North Nova Scotia Highlanders during training in the United Kingdom. The carrier has the CT series number of a Canadian Army vehicle and the diamond device with MT presumably indicates the mortar troop. In a real combat situation it is unlikely that the carrier would remain so close to the weapon when it was firing.

one per battery in the summer of 1940, later increased to one per troop, before taking delivery of what they refer to as a 'specially-fitted version' – Carrier Armoured Observation Post – at some later date.

The next batch, designated Carrier AOP Mark III, began with a big contract for 3,443 in September 1941 followed by two smaller orders in 1943, all from Ford at Dagenham. The Mark III had a crew of four and an additional cable reel at the front. First-hand accounts of their use are not easy to find. They were certainly still in service in 1944, yet even at the time of the desert war it is clear that many regiments preferred modified tanks for this work. A summary of experience in France, compiled at the end of the war, claims that the AOP Carrier was unpopular with self-propelled artillery regiments because it had inadequate capacity, was vulnerable and was too slow to keep up with heavier vehicles on long journeys.

Medium Machine-gun Carriers

In 1943 the organization of the infantry division underwent one of its periodic convulsions with the creation of the Brigade Support Group. Based on recent experience, there was a desire to increase the firepower available at brigade level with medium (Vickers) machine guns for volume, 4.2in mortars for high explosive and 20mm automatic weapons for low-level anti-aircraft defence and the ability to tackle light armoured vehicles. Army Training Instruction No. 7 provided the details, evidently unaware that to some extent it had just reinvented the wheel.

Universal Carriers would play a major part in the new organization, with 30 of them in all in each brigade support group, three of which combined to form a support battalion. Events had gone virtually full circle, since these carriers would be modified to carry a Vickers machine gun, and this is where we came in. However, this modified carrier was not identical with the original Machine Gun Carrier: the gun would not be carried in the front of the vehicle but on a modified mounting fitted to the top of the carrier's engine cover. The medium machine-gun company in the support group was divided into three platoons, each of which was equipped with four carriers armed with machine guns. Each carrier had a four-man crew and 19 factory-packed spools of ammunition, each spool of 250 rounds (4,750 rounds in all). A No. 22 radio was provided for each platoon but whether it was carried in a carrier or not is unclear. Some things did not change. The intention, quite clearly, was to operate the weapon dismounted whenever possible, although it could be fired from the vehicle in a direct-fire role over the heads of friendly infantry. Firing on the move was not encouraged other than in exceptional circumstances.

The heavy mortar company had two platoons, each of eight weapons, but at the time the Training Instruction was written it was clear that the mortars would be carried in 15cwt trucks. The intention was, apparently, to provide Universal Carriers and trailers but, in the event, the larger Canadian-built Windsor Carrier was adopted for this role and it could manage without a trailer.

The 20mm cannon of the Anti-Aircraft Company was subdivided into four platoons, each of four guns. These could be Oerlikon, Polsten or

A Universal Carrier Mark I with everything laid out for inspection and crew members in place. In a small vehicle such as this, efficiency requires that these items are stowed to plan so that everyone knows where they are. To this end the War Office produced a series of special stowage diagrams, which, in the case of carriers, cover most primary roles. Note in particular the Bren gun, Boys rifle and signal flags.

A Mark II Universal in the process of conversion to a Medium Machine Gun Carrier with all the new fittings still in primer paint, in particular the pedestal mount and ammunition holder on top of the engine and the stowage bracket for the Vickers gun to the left, in the compartment behind the driver.

Hispano-Suiza. The 1943 document has nothing whatever to say about transport where these guns are concerned and the only reason for mentioning them is a comment in the book *With The Jocks* in which the author mentions 20mm guns hauled by carriers. It would be expecting too much that he should specify which type and, in the absence of other sources, it could be anything from Universals and Loyds to T16 or Windsor.

Invasion

Amphibious operations present armies with all manner of additional problems, not least of which is the transfer of vehicles from ship to shore without getting wet, or at least wet in the wrong places. As early as September 1941 MEE ran a series of tests, running a carrier in a 3ft (91cm) deep tank. With all apertures sealed it was discovered that a carrier could keep running for up to two and a half minutes in very calm water before things started to go wrong. Even so there were peculiar problems. For example, the man sitting next to the driver was advised to hold a seat cushion over the Bren gun aperture as the vehicle took the plunge, to stop water from pouring in. Water found its way in anyway and MEE recommended the development of a quick-acting drain plug to let it all out again as soon as the vehicle reached dry land. A succession of landing operations from 1942 built up a mass of experience and by 1944, when preparations were being made to invade France, waterproofing techniques were all tried and tested. Instructions for the landings included a requirement that all vehicles sent across the Channel between 6 June and 18 July (D+42) must be fully waterproofed.

The task was carried out at unit level, by crews, and involved hours of work with various types of sticky compound sealing every gap and joint that might let water in. A vehicle's engine was clearly the most sensitive part. It must have access to air but exclude moisture from all electrical components and, from the carrier point of view, it is unfortunate that

REME, who masterminded the whole process, regarded the Ford V8 as their greatest challenge. The carrier was further handicapped by its low overall height and open top. Under normal circumstances, with modest preparation, a Universal Carrier could drive through calm water up to 2ft 3in (68.5cm) deep but for Normandy, and indeed Salerno the previous year, deep wading up to 5ft (1.5m) was required to account for waves and an uneven sea bed. This was only achieved by effectively doubling the height of the body using extra steel panels held in place by a system of rods and brackets. Naturally, once this was done the driver could not see a thing, so he had to be directed by the vehicle commander peering over the top. Once ashore, the driver knocked out a small panel to give himself some view and, as soon as time could be spared, the extension panels were removed. The entire waterproofing process, with diagrams, was laid out in a pamphlet issued by the Ministry of Supply.

Canadian troops with an MMG Carrier in Italy, with the Vickers gun and ammunition box in place. T 43261 was a Canadian-built Mark I stripped of all tinwork but with personalized stowage arrangements and non-standard headlights. Red/white/red stripes on the side were an Allied identification sign in Italy.

A typical example of an infantry battalion on D-Day itself might be 1st Battalion the Suffolk Regiment. The troops crossed the Channel in four LSI (Landing Ship Infantry) while the anti-tank, mortar and carrier platoons were distributed among three LCT (Landing Craft Tank). Nothing is recorded as to how the carriers fared during the landing but on 9 June a carrier was hit by a round from an 88mm gun and the commanding officer, Lieutenant-Colonel R. E. Goodwin, badly wounded. Meanwhile on Juno Beach Lieutenant-Colonel Reeves, acting in the role of official observer, watched in horror as a Universal Carrier, already wilting under the weight of its deep wading gear, staggered ashore filled to the top with additional stores and struggling to tow a 6-pdr anti-tank gun. With the driver's foot to the floor it slipped continually on the coir matting beneath it while smoke poured from the overheated brakes.

Inland, 61st Reconnaissance Regiment, acting on behalf of 50th (Northumberland) Division at the time, was operating in a communication role. A carrier patrol, accompanied by the commanding officer, missed a recall signal and entered a village from the 'wrong' side while a battle was raging between British tanks and German infantry. To the utter amazement of the tank men the little carrier column drove straight through the middle of the fight, with the CO standing upright in the leading carrier, and passed upon its way unscathed.

Few regimental histories have much to say about carriers in North-West Europe; they are there, in the background, but rarely warrant more than a passing mention. First Battalion the Dorsetshire Regiment, for example, tells how, soon after D-Day on a major move across the front when changing brigades, the carriers and mortars formed a piquet along the route of march. Later in June, during the advance to Villers-Bocage, the battalion found itself overlooked by German tanks on a hill and flanked by infantry on another eminence, making it difficult to bring up anti-tank guns. As a last resort carriers were used to tow the 6-pdrs. and even risked crossing a minefield, only to have all the carriers get bogged down.

Far East

A rare example of carriers being used by United States forces occurred in the wake of the Japanese attack on the Philippines, when a Canadian ship, the *Don Jose*, remained stranded in Manila harbour and at General MacArthur's request the cargo was made available to the Americans. It consisted of motor transport and 57 Universal Carriers intended for two Canadian motor battalions in Hong Kong. Forty were handed over to a Colonel Weaver, commanding a Provisional Tank Group, and armed locally. They did not last very long. Japanese snipers soon picked off the crews of these open-topped vehicles, revealing once again their inherent vulnerability.

The Japanese assault on Singapore gave rise to at least one action involving carriers. Arriving without their own carriers, which had been lost at sea, 4th Battalion the Suffolk Regiment acquired five, described inevitably as Bren Gun Carriers, from a vehicle park. More carriers could be seen in the park but five was all they were allowed. These were apparently covered over with wire netting to keep grenades out and referred to by the men as Chicken Coops. The carrier platoon took part in an attack against Japanese positions on an eminence known as Swiss Rifle Club Hill on the afternoon of 11 February 1942. It was a dismounted attack and soon repulsed.

Other uses

In July 1941 MEE staged a comparative trial between a Universal Carrier and a Loyd acting as a tractor for the 2-pdr anti-tank gun. There was no question over the ability of the vehicles to handle the gun and this trial was merely intended to discover which was best – it showed that there was no appreciable difference.

Army Training Memorandum (ATM) No. 48, issued in May 1944, announced that in future all Universal Carriers, but not OP Carriers, would be supplied with an item known as the Stacey towing attachment. Others would be issued to selected units for fitting to existing carriers. The Stacey attachment was a heavy-duty sprung towing hook that bolted to the rear plate of a carrier and the purpose was the emergency towing

A Mark II Universal fully prepared for wading. In addition to the raised panels there is evidence of sealant having been applied around all joints and even rivet heads, of a canvas cover over the driver's visor and of extra protection around the gun aperture and headlamp.

Polish troops and their Mark II MMG Carrier prepare for a ferry ride across the river Seine during the advance across France. The ferry, which is hauled across by cable, is assembled from lightweight trackway supported on two folding boat pontoons.

of the 6-pdr anti-tank gun – and the memorandum stressed emergency. It was intended, said the ATM, 'to tow a 6-pr A tk gun (but not a 25-pr gun), in an emergency, over short distances'.

The 6-pdr weighed 2,471lbs (1.1 tonnes) complete, which placed quite a strain upon the towing vehicle and indeed the towing attachment itself but, regrettably, this injunction not to overdo it was often ignored. The sight of carriers towing two-wheel trailers in France suggests that the towing attachment found other uses.

In 1941 various changes were introduced in the organization of an infantry division. One concerned the old Divisional Cavalry Regiment as used in France, and its replacement by a Divisional Reconnaissance Battalion. In other words from now on the infantry would take care of their own reconnaissance and not rely upon the Royal Armoured Corps.

The organization was complicated. The battalion comprised three reconnaissance companies, each of which consisted of an infantry platoon, carried in light trucks, and three scout platoons. This is what concerns us. The scout platoon was divided into three sections, one of which had five light reconnaissance cars (Beaverettes, later Humbers) and two sections each having three Universal Carriers with appropriate stowage arrangements. These were to be administered by a new formation, the Reconnaissance Corps.

In fact the Recce Corps, as it came to be known, did not always conform to its establishment table. Many units acquired armoured cars (which they referred to as 'heavies') and in the Far East some worked entirely on foot. In January 1944 the Reconnaissance Corps, while retaining its title, became part of the Royal Armoured Corps. The terminology changed from battalion to regiment, from company to squadron and from platoon to troop but the establishment was largely unchanged. Universal Carriers remained a significant part. A similar arrangement prevailed in the case of an airborne division which had Universal Carriers in its armoured reconnaissance regiment. The three troops of each squadron included two carriers and two Jeeps while six more carriers formed two troops of the support squadron. Universal Carriers were airportable in the Hamilcar glider.

A number of photographs show Universal Carriers employed as stretcher carriers, operating under the Red Cross flag. It would be inaccurate to describe them as ambulances since in the main they appear to be unmodified vehicles with two stretchers laid fore and aft either side

Lifting the Ford V8 engine out of a Canadian-built Mark I Carrier in Holland. A twin boom wrecker is used as the hoist and the work is being carried out by the Royal Canadian Electrical and Mechanical Engineers. There are not many armoured vehicles that could be stripped of an engine this easily.

of the engine but above the armour. It must have resulted in a very uncomfortable ride for the casualties and, since no special brackets were provided, the crews were obliged to hold the stretchers in place. Ambulance carriers did exist and invariably mounted a canvas canopy.

The Universal Carrier was, by its very nature and ubiquity, adapted to dozens of different, unofficial roles too numerous to list even if they were all known. As it is, one can only rely on surviving photographs or vague descriptions, two of which must suffice to give the general picture. In at least one instance a Universal Carrier was equipped with cable-laying equipment more commonly seen in specially adapted versions of the Loyd Carrier. Reports indicate that carriers were tested in 1943 with a device for laying smoke screens but, unfortunately, few details survive.

FIREPOWER

There are many things that a soldier can never have enough of. In combat two in particular are firepower and protection. There were few opportunities to improve the latter, where carriers were concerned, although a few more filled sandbags across the front never went amiss, but when it came to weaponry the world was the carrier man's oyster. Given the general belief that other people's weapons are better than one's own it is not surprising to find odd examples of everything from a captured German MG42, or appropriated American .50 Browning to, in at least one case, a big 20mm Solothurn cannon sprouting from different carriers but here we must limit ourselves to more official projects.

One scheme was to turn carriers (or turretless light tanks if available) into tank destroyers along the lines of motor torpedo boats on land. A modified carrier would carry one thick slab of armour at the front and, above the engine at the rear, a turntable supporting four gun tubes. These barrels would be laid side by side, able to rotate on the turntable and capable of ten degrees of elevation. No particular gun is specified but, given the date, 57mm 6-pdrs. would be likely.

This unusual photograph shows Universal Carriers acting as troop transports in Burma. The nearest vehicle has at least ten men aboard, including the driver; the second has a spare strip of carrier track masking the weapon aperture. All three have what seems to be a folding stretcher attached to the side and appear to be worn, battered and close to collapse.

In the chaos of a desert tank melee, these small but highly manoeuvrable vehicles would dash in among the German tanks and shoot them up. Each pre-loaded gun would be fired electrically and, once fired, would slide backwards off the turntable and fall to the ground, to be collected later. Once the thing had fired off all four barrels it would retire from the fight, presumably to reload. No doubt a generation of carrier men sighed with relief at the fact that it was never tried.

This is not to say, however, that all daft ideas died at the drawing board stage. Witness the Smith Gun. The eponymous designer was said to be an engineer working for a toy company but, be that as it may, he rapidly designed a lightweight, 3in gun, soon after the fall of France. It entered production, notwithstanding that its ammunition had been condemned as dangerous to the user by almost everyone who inspected it. Most went to the Home Guard but the Army and Royal Air Force had a few for airfield defence; how one ever got to be mounted in a carrier is anyone's guess.

The chosen prototype seems to have been a Bren Gun Carrier but no serial numbers can be seen on any surviving photographs and the hull has been modified sufficiently to make precise identification impossible. The armour was a lot higher at the front, primarily to accommodate the gun, but this provided improved protection for the driver as well. One suspects internal modifications also, otherwise it would be very difficult to load the weapon, but there are no photographs surviving to clarify this. The Smith Gun was a smooth-bore piece firing a high explosive shell or a High Explosive Anti-Tank (HEAT) round (capable of penetrating

Mark I Universals of the Reconnaissance Corps on a winter exercise in the north of England, probably early in 1944. The vehicle in the foreground is unusual since it has a PIAT anti-tank weapon mounted where the Bren gun should be.

about 60mm of armour) to a range of about 500yd (450m). Needless to say, demonstration of the carrier prototype did not lead to production.

In 1943 MEE was asked to test a new mounting for the PIAT (Projector, Infantry, Anti-Tank), a crude, hand-held weapon fired by a large spring. It was required to mount the weapon on a carrier on brackets above the gunner's armour, facing forwards, and MEE was to see if it would stay in place, already loaded, when the vehicle was driven across country. Extended trials revealed that the weapon hardly suffered at all but that it was impossible to keep the projectile in place. It became dislodged, and potentially lethal, at the first bump. The logic behind its use is difficult to comprehend. The PIAT had an effective range of just 100yd (90m) and the chances of an enemy tank permitting a carrier to get that close are too slim to be worth worrying about.

Not that this prevented the Canadians from going one, or perhaps we should say thirteen better. Their idea mounted fourteen PIATs, arranged in two rows of seven, on a special framework at the rear of some carriers in North-West Europe. One could fire either seven, or all fourteen, at a time using a very basic system of rods and levers but once again it meant getting suicidally close to the target with just the slight advantage over the British design that the carrier was facing the right way for a quick escape if things went awry.

One of the Canadian contracts includes a batch of 100 carriers described as Tank Hunters. This presumably refers to a Canadian variant that carried a 2-pdr anti-tank gun, complete with shield, on a rotating mount at the forward end of the engine compartment. As such modifications go, it appears neat and compact, but Canadian sources suggest that only two dozen were built and, apart from one sent to Britain for trials, the remainder were employed for airfield defence in western Canada.

Posed in the nose of a Hamilcar glider, this Mark II Universal has just reversed aboard up the special ramps. The photograph was taken during preparations for Operation Plunder, the Rhine Crossing of March 1945. Once the nose door is shut and the vehicle secured, the aircraft will be ready for take-off.

An artist's impression of the bizarre tank destroyers, based on Universal Carriers. By the look of it, at least in the designer's imagination, they appear to have disabled a complete Panzer regiment. Designed by Mr Louis Motley of Hydran Products, it was offered to the Gunnery School at Lulworth in July 1942.

POST-WAR ACTIVITIES

When the war ended, vast numbers of carriers were in service in every theatre. By rights, they should all have been scrapped as obsolete, but instead many were retained in service. Preference would have been given to the larger, more modern types from North America, the Windsor and T16. However, in 1948, when the British Army changed over to a new numbering system, hundreds of Universals were still being used. Indeed, they saw active service with the Commonwealth Division during the Korean War.

Others were used for experimental purposes, not necessarily in connection with subsequent carrier development but simply because they were available. One was tested by SADE (Specialised Armour Development Establishment) with a pair of rockets strapped to each side which, when fired, enabled the carrier to extricate itself from a muddy hole. Another, fitted with more rockets, was supposed to jump across gaps. Yet another was modified at FVRDE (Fighting Vehicle Research & Development Establishment) with additional fittings that enabled it to be run at different ground pressures over a variety of surfaces. Oddest of all was a well-protected carrier, equipped with a powerful water jet that was used to unearth buried mines on British beaches now that the threat of invasion was removed. Mystery still surrounds a batch of carriers that were apparently armoured all over, with raised sides and a roof. They were photographed in a British scrapyard but so far no explanation has been forthcoming.

Many more were supplied to other armies. The Irish Army had in fact acquired more than 200 carriers during the war and these remained in service into the 1960s. In March 1956 the British Government presented 100 Universal Carriers to the German Army. The Danish Army fitted some of their carriers with 106mm recoilless anti-tank weapons covered by a sort of tubular steel and canvas superstructure. Egyptian carriers confronted their former owners at Suez in 1956 and many ended up with the Israeli Army during the Middle East wars. In fact there can have been few armies, large or small, that could not produce at least some carriers in the post-war years.

The Smith Gun Carrier, a one-off conversion prompted by the invasion scare in Britain, following the fall of France. The additional armour suggests a lot of extra weight at the front. Despite the fact that the Smith Gun was never used in action it is credited, because of the unstable nature of its ammunition, with killing far too many of its own crews.

Despite this world-wide use, hundreds of British Army carriers went to the scrap heap as they were phased out of service. This was quite literally the case in some instances and small mountains of them could be seen, waiting to be broken up. A few were sold out of service for industrial use but they tended to be more trouble than they were worth, in terms both of fuel consumption and of maintenance. Those that survived are now almost all in private hands, the ideal restoration project for anyone who wishes to own a full-tracked armoured vehicle that is relatively easy to maintain and transport. Preserved examples are tangible pieces of history – and everyone still refers to them as Bren Gun Carriers!

BIBLIOGRAPHY

Chamberlain, P., and C. Ellis, *Making Tracks*, Profile Publications Ltd, 1973

Ellis, Major L. F., *Welsh Guards at War*, Gale and Polden, 1946

Fletcher, David, *Mechanised Force: British Tanks between the Wars*, HMSO, 1991

Fletcher, David, *The Great Tank Scandal: British Armour in the Second World War, Part 1*, HMSO, 1989

Fletcher, David, *The Universal Tank: British Armour in the Second World War, Part 2*, HMSO, 1993

The Vickers Tanks from Landships to Challenger 2, Keepdate Publishing Ltd, 1995

White, B. T., *British Tanks and Fighting Vehicles 1914–1945*, Ian Allan, 1970

Zaloga, S., *Blitzkrieg: Armour Camouflage and Markings 1939–1940*, Arms & Armour Press, 1980

The Canadian 2-pdr anti-tank carrier, based upon a Mark I Universal, gives every appearance of being a sound and potentially effective design although it was never used in combat. Note the ammunition stowage arrangements inside the hull.

A1: MACHINE GUN CARRIER NO. 2 MARK I, 2ND BATTALION THE CHESHIRE REGIMENT, C.1937

The Cheshire Regiment, whose cap badge is also shown, was no stranger to mechanization. This 2nd Battalion provided a motorized infantry element for the 1927 Experimental Armoured Force and in subsequent years employed the troublesome little Carden-Loyd Carriers. Designated a machine gun battalion and equipped with Machine Gun Carriers, it would have exchanged these for 15cwt platoon trucks once the Bren gun was introduced. In peacetime, when appearances counted for more than camouflage, the vehicle would have been finished in a glossy dark green and decorated with the regimental badge and battalion title. The large, red letter A indicates a front-line, combat vehicle; other types carried a B. The War Office census number was the carrier's primary identification but, between the wars, military vehicles were also required to display a civilian-style registration plate, invariably in sequences issued by the County of Middlesex.

A2: SCOUT CARRIER OF 4TH/7TH ROYAL DRAGOON GUARDS, SECOND DIVISION, BRITISH EXPEDITIONARY FORCE, FRANCE, 1940

Scout Carriers were issued to those divisional cavalry regiments that provided the armoured reconnaissance element for British infantry divisions. There were seven such regiments in France, each one equipped with 28 Light Tanks and 44 Scout Carriers. The Cross Keys insignia of Second Infantry Division, to which the 4th/7th Dragoon Guards was attached, was displayed on the right front mudguard. The figure 2, in white on a black plate, identified the vehicle as belonging to the divisional cavalry regiment of the formation concerned. If the vehicle was out of action this plate could be reversed in its holder, revealing the word

Mark I Universal Carriers of the Irish Army photographed in 1942. The riflemen in the back have probably been added by the photographer to impress the uninitiated. It seems very unlikely that they could be expected to hit anything with the vehicle in motion.

'PASS'. Most BEF vehicles still retained their civil registration plates at this time, although they were later painted over. British armoured vehicles in France were painted in so-called khaki green with a disruptive pattern of dark green. The No. 11 Wireless Set, introduced in 1938, was regarded as a short-range, general purpose radio for use in vehicles and as a ground station.

B1: BREN GUN CARRIER, 4TH INDIAN DIVISION, EGYPT, 1940

A set of publicity photographs, taken at the time they were training, shows 4th Indian Division Bren Gun Carriers in a basic light sand colour, over-painted with blobs of a darker hue that is believed to be brown. The markings are unusual and painted in a way that suggests advertisement, rather than information. The impressive red eagle motif of the division is larger than War Office instructions allow, as is the arm of service marking, which raises problems of its own. The number 311 is difficult to explain. It does not conform to known practice and the only context in which 300 series numbers were used in the Middle East appears to have been with the Australian Imperial Force, which seems unlikely. Indeed it may well be that all of these signs were painted on, larger than life, for publicity purposes so the number, colour and locations could be meaningless.

Notice the bridging disc, also painted larger than life on the right side, and the way that the WD number is emblazoned on the front like a registration plate. This number is repeated correctly on the left side of the vehicle. The weapon is a Mark I Bren gun.

B2: UNIVERSAL CARRIER X SQUADRON (1RGH) YEOMANRY ARMOURED DETACHMENT, GB, 1941

The armoured roof, with its stout, angle iron supports, must have made the interior of the carrier somewhat claustrophobic, not to mention difficult to load or get out of in a hurry. No accounts survive as to the extra weight or how that affected performance. Anti-aircraft fire was impossible but it seems that the Boys rifle was the favoured weapon for the front mounting.

It is not easy to interpret the markings. The number 51 is seen on many of the vehicles and this is assumed to be on a green background since all three regiments that supplied squadrons to the YAD belonged to 20th Armoured Brigade in more normal times and this was an independent brigade until October 1940. Squadron signs are also in evidence but, in the surviving photographs only the triangle and square, which may be taken to represent X and Y squadrons, are known. If so, then the triangle should represent 1st Royal Gloucestershire Hussars. One photograph shows a set of superimposed triangles on the offside mudguard but it is impossible to determine the colours. It is known that 1st RGH chose local county names for their vehicles but all that can be read from the photograph is ****lingham; *Arlingham* is suggested as a reasonable possibility.

C1: CARRIER MARK II, 1ST ROYAL IRISH FUSILIERS, 38TH IRISH BRIGADE, 78TH INFANTRY DIVISION, ITALY, 1943

Known as the Battleaxe Division, the 78th had a distinguished fighting record from the landings in Tunisia to the end of the war in Italy. The 38th Brigade, which joined the Division in March 1943, comprised three battalions with strong Irish connections. The carrier is stowed for the second-in-command of a carrier platoon and is fitted with a 2in mortar (also shown separately) to the left of the fighting compartment. Thirty rounds for this weapon were stowed on the left side at the rear and included a selection of small star shells with different coloured arrays. The frame on the rear of the engine cover is a folded tripod for the Bren Gun.

If surviving photographs are any guide, the extra set of steps above the rear bogie on each side rarely lasted long in service.

C2: UNIVERSAL CARRIER AMBULANCE, 2ND NEW ZEALAND DIVISION, ITALY, 1943

Painted white and sporting a weatherproof canopy marked with red crosses, in addition to a Red Cross flag, this vehicle served with a Royal Army Medical Corps unit of 2nd New Zealand Division in Italy and shows the well-known Fern Leaf sign. Many sources suggest that these Ambulance carriers were modified by removing the rear hull panel so that stretchers could be loaded from the back; on this example the side panel seems to have been extended to improve protection. It would be difficult to imagine any other way of loading stretchers quickly with the canopy in place. A stowage locker has been attached at the front and a rack for Jerrycans alongside the driver.

Conditions in Italy, particularly the mountainous north, favoured the use of carriers for work such as this. They could reach places where no wheeled ambulance could hope to go. They also offered more protection than a conventional ambulance although they must have been extremely uncomfortable.

D: UNIVERSAL CARRIER MARK II

In mechanical terms the Universal Carrier employs basic lorry technology of the period. The Ford V8 engine, which is water-cooled with the radiator in the bulkhead in front of it, drives back through a standard clutch to a four-speed and reverse gearbox which is also straight off the Ford production line. This in turn passes drive to a standard Ford differential driving axle and, via conventional drum brakes, to the drive sprockets.

Where it differs from a wheeled vehicle is in the steering system, although the controls, in the driver's position, would all be familiar to a lorry driver apart from the fact that the steering wheel is vertical. Turning the steering wheel in either

A Mark II Universal in post-war guise acting as tractor for a 6-pdr anti-tank gun. In 1948 the British Army introduced a new numbering system, based on a sequence of two digits, two letters, two digits, to replace the old T series. This served as a vehicle identification number and the equivalent of a civil registration plate, even if it was not always painted across the front.

A Universal Carrier of the Middlesex Regiment towing an American trailer in Korea. Both carrier and trailer appear to be well laden but the vehicle is also carrying a Soviet Maxim machine gun, complete with shield, located on top of the engine cover.

direction causes the main suspension cross tube to shift laterally, moving the suspension units and displacing the track, which, when curved as shown, initiates a turn. In a tight corner the driver pulls the wheel over harder, applies more power and, by applying the brake on one side of the differential or the other, enables the vehicle to make a skid turn.

Track links are short-pitch, single-pin in malleable cast iron with double guide horns. Track tension is maintained by adjusting the front idler wheels on their brackets while the suspension system operates on double coil springs.

E1: THREE-INCH MORTAR CARRIER, THE ROYAL WINNIPEG RIFLES, 3RD CANADIAN INFANTRY DIVISION, UK

A bird's-eye view of a fully stowed Three-Inch Mortar Carrier in Canadian Army service. Third Canadian Infantry Division, whose identifying mark was a simple, French grey rectangle, landed over Juno Beach on D-Day. As the senior regiment in the senior (7th Canadian Infantry) brigade the Royal Winnipeg Rifles display 55 on a red square.

On the move the mortar tube is carried across the back, encased within a special container, along with its tripod, while the base-plate sits at the front. The interior is given over as much as possible to ammunition stowage, which is not a pleasant cargo. Although it is not shown here, the stowage diagrams reveal that on selected Mortar Carriers a No. 18 wireless set was mounted at the front, where the Bren gun might go. A 3in mortar is also shown in firing mode.

E2: UNIVERSAL CARRIER , 9TH INFANTRY BRIGADE, 3RD INFANTRY DIVISION, EQUIPPED FOR DEEP WADING, D-DAY 6 JUNE 1944

British 3rd Infantry Division, the Iron Division, came ashore over Sword Beach on D-Day. This illustration represents a Universal Carrier of 1st Battalion the King's Own Scottish Borderers in 9th Infantry Brigade on that day. The green- coloured square symbolizes the second brigade in the division while the number 61 indicates the second regiment in the brigade.

Five-pointed white stars served as a recognition sign for all Allied armies at this time, not just the Americans.

Deep wading screens surround the entire hull, locked in place by metal rods, keyed to brackets welded to the hull. Gaps between these plates, and indeed any other joints and openings, were thickly sealed with sticky compounds such as Bostick. Preparing any vehicle for wading was both messy and time-consuming yet it had to be done with the utmost care if the vehicle was not to be drowned as it struggled ashore from its landing craft.

F1: AOP CARRIER MARK II , 1ST BATTERY, 69TH FIELD REGIMENT, 49TH INFANTRY DIVISION, NORMANDY, 1944

With its Polar Bear insignia evoking an association with Iceland, 49th (West Riding) Division landed in Normandy as part of the second wave. Other markings on this Armoured Observation Post Carrier indicate the battery commander's vehicle (white X) of the first Battery (red square in top right-hand corner of larger blue square) of the senior field regiment (number 42) of the division.

The vehicle is shown re-stowed to an arrangement introduced in December 1943 which included an extending ladder and other long items strapped to the side. Although the wide slot at the front, intended to accommodate a set of binoculars, is a particular identifying feature of the AOP Carrier the main business of this type is communication. Hence the reel of signal cable mounted at the front (there is another at the back) and the profusion of radio aerial mounts for No. 18 and No. 19 sets around the hull. The main radio, the classic No. 19 wireless set, is shown separately. A short- range signalling lamp is also carried.

F2: MEDIUM MACHINE GUN CARRIER, 1ST BATTALION THE MIDDLESEX REGIMENT, 15TH SCOTTISH DIVISION, NORTH-WEST EUROPE, 1944

In a division where all regiments in all three infantry brigades were Scots, 1st Battalion the Middlesex Regiment might have stuck out like a sore thumb. Yet it had been the division's support battalion since October 1943, converting to the new role of machine gun battalion in March 1944. The carrier displays the division's lion rampant insignia and the number 64 on a black arm of service square, indicating divisional troops.

The Vickers machine gun, with its distinctive bell-mouthed muzzle attachment, is situated above the engine, facing forwards. When not required, the weapon was stowed in the special bracket in the compartment behind the driver, with the tripod on the opposite side. Spare ammunition boxes are stowed on both sides. Notice that an extra set of pioneer tools, to be used when digging-in the gun, are located to the front.

G: UNIVERSAL CARRIERS MARK I*, FORD FACTORY, WINDSOR, ONTARIO, 1942

Canada established a branch of the Ford Motor Company in 1903, just one year after Henry Ford set up his original factory in the United States. Early in the Second World War, Ford of Canada teamed up with General Motors of Canada to produce a range of military lorries under the Canadian Military Pattern title which were produced for Britain and other Commonwealth allies.

Production of Universal Carriers was undertaken entirely by Fords, using the inevitable production-line basis pioneered by Henry Ford himself. Once problems in the production of armour plate had been resolved, manufacture got under way on a massive scale and, although sources differ, there is no doubt that around 30,000 Universals were completed before the plant switched to producing the larger Windsor model. This artwork is based to some extent on a painting of carriers being assembled at Ford's Dagenham plant in Britain since the manufacturing process was nearly enough identical.

G2: UNIVERSAL CARRIER MARK I, SPECIALISED ARMOUR DEVELOPMENT ESTABLISHMENT, WOODBRIDGE, SUFFOLK, JULY 1946

Rocket assisted take-off: SADE evolved from the wartime 79th Armoured Division – from whom it inherited the famous bull's head insignia – when the latter was disbanded in 1945. SADE was dedicated to undertaking a great variety of experiments that had their genesis in wartime concepts. Rocket-assisted egress was one such.

It had been developed in order to help propel DD amphibious tanks up muddy river banks and was subsequently expanded as a general means of un-ditching bogged vehicles. It relied on quick-burning rockets, originally designed to get aircraft airborne on short runways, and, at least in these early trials, seems to have functioned perfectly well. Redundant Universal Carriers were used for a number of SADE experiments simply because they were available. T208941 carried the unit insignia on its left front track guard and the letter A – in black on a white square – for A Wing, on the right.

Abandoned by its current owners, a Universal Carrier of the Egyptian Army is examined by British troops during the 1956 Suez Crisis. Improvised sand shields, running full length, have been added behind the original valances.

Danish troops with an extensively modified Mark II Universal. The weapon could be a 106mm recoilless anti-tank gun or simply a length of tube which, in conjunction with the canvas screen, might be intended to represent a turreted tank for training purposes.

INDEX